BAMBURGH

Bamburgh is a quiet and pretty seaside village built in the form of a triangle around a grove of trees which take the place of a village green. The castle forms the apex of the triangle.

The population today is small but in early times it was more numerous. In Saxon times the village was situated on the rock covering what is now the west and east wards of the castle, but certain buildings must have been outside the fortress precincts, like the church of St Aidan which stood on the site of the present parish church.

The importance of the town in the 12th century can be judged from the contribution of over £18 which it made to the Royal Exchequer in 1177. In the following century Henry III granted a charter to the township in which "our honest men of Bamburgh for a fee of 26 marks of silver to be paid annually at Easter", were freed from the jurisdiction of the sheriff and allowed their own customs and local laws.

The town continued to prosper and in the year 1295 the burgesses sent two members to the 'Model Parliament' of Edward I. The two members were John de Greystanes and William le Coroner. The only other places in Northumberland which were represented in Parliament were Corbridge and Newcastle. This was the only occasion Bamburgh sent members to London.

above - Medieval dovecote at Bamburgh

left - Gateway to the castle garden

opposite page - Clock tower at Bamburgh Castle

In the following year a special subsidy or capital tax was levied by the king and 28 burgesses paid the subsidy, contributing nearly £4. The names of the contributors are given and provide an interesting list of the most important inhabitants in those times. Here they are :

Master of the Hospital
Henry the son of Gregory
Robert Roter
Stephan the son of Radulf
Robert Scarf
Henry the Alblaster
William Gray
Ada Pelliparius
Thomas Marescall
Stephan Narus
William the Barker
John of Graystanes
John Cher
W. Sneke
Robert of Heuedrow
William the Coroner
John Mayle
Margaret the widow of Robert Gystanes
John the son of John Mayle
Gilbert Goldewyn
William the son of John
Peter of Castro
William Anham
William the son of Reginald
Walter the son of Mayn
Alice the widow of Robert Godman
William Cotus
Ada Porter

Hardly was the tax paid, however, before the town was laid waste by the Scots in 1297. In the 14th century the town recovered and we are told there were 120 burgesses. There was a market place marked by a cross, the base of which can still be seen at the west end of the village green. Near the market cross were the stocks and a cucking-stool. The town drew its water from three wells called Edynwell (St Aidan's well), Wydnewell (the well in the Wynding) and Maudeleynwell. The harbour for the town was at Warenmouth.

In the following century further Scottish raids reduced the town to poverty and the burgesses were unable to pay the taxes which in consequence had to be reduced. The town never recovered from these Scottish incursions and the devastation caused by the Wars of the Roses. But they soon had revenge on the Scots. In 1472 the magnificent barge of the Bishop of St Andrews, called the *St Salvador*, when returning from Flanders richly laden with merchandise, was wrecked off Bamburgh. The cargo was quickly plundered and the Abbot of St Columbane, who was a passenger, was taken prisoner, and was released after a ransom of £80 was paid.

The Copper Kettle, Bamburgh

As the town declined the Master of the Austin canons, who had an establishment in the town, was able to seize all the lands and houses in the borough and the municipality ceased to exist. With the dissolution of the monasteries the village came into the hands of the Forster family. At the end of the 16th century Sir John Forster was warden of the Middle Marches which he administered very well. When he died in 1602 he left the sum of £1,020, a large amount for those days, but of this more than half was spent on his funeral. Such extravagance on a funeral was characteristic of the times. Some of the items on which the money was spent are of great interest. Here is a selection :

	£	s	d
For the herald	57	4	8
For the preacher	5	0	0
Spice at Newcastle and bankettinge stuffe	18	8	6
Thirteen gallons of sack	2	0	0
Three hogsheads of wine	16	10	0

	£	s	d
Seven stone of butter at 4 shillings a stone	1	8	0
Birds from the Farnes		10	0
Hops (for brewing)	1	15	4
Ten turkeys	2	5	0
21 pigs		17	8
12 dozen chickens	1	14	0

And so on, the food is listed for the funeral feast. The largest item, however, is for mourning black clothes. They are mentioned several times, one charge alone being £158.

We mention in the next chapter how the lands of the Forsters came into the possession of Lord Crewe and eventually to the charity he endowed. Dr John Sharp one of the most famous of the trustees described as follows some of the work done by the Crewe Charity.

North Gateway, Bamburgh Castle

"I succeeded him in the trust. The children wanted education, therefore schools were necessary: and where so proper as under the eye of the trustees? The rights of the latter were suffering from want of manor courts being held, to remedy which a court room was fitted up, where courts are held regularly twice a year. On my brother's death I succeeded to the living; and as he left me his library, I sold it to the trustees in order to its being made a public library. The poor on this maritime coast were frequently much distressed for want of corn. This grievance was alleviated by the erection of granaries. Once a vessel was wrecked behind the castle and the crew saved; but the unfortunate master, having escaped the perils of the sea, died of a damp bed in the village. That, the like might never happen again, all shipwrecked sailors who come are received here and supplied with every necessary. This was the beginning of our little infirmary, which soon suggested the idea of a general dispensary for the poor, which is particularly useful in this part of the country as there is no other charity of the kind between Edinbro and Newcastle. The vicinity of the Fern Islands and the want of regular soundings without them, pointed out the convenience of regular firing in a fog; and an old gun, found in the sand, was applied to that purpose, which has answered our most sanguine expectations. The accidental discovery of the ancient well pointed out the convenience of baths, and the infirmary required a variety of them. The number of wrecks on this particular coast of vessels that had run for Holy Island harbour in a storm and failed of getting into it, and the melancholy sights from the castle of persons wrecked on the islands and starving with cold and hunger together with the savage plundering of such goods as were driven on shore, induced the lords of the manor to give every assistance to vessels in distress, and premiums for saving of lives."

Entrance to the keep at Bamburgh Castle

BAMBURGH CASTLE

"With its main outline hardly marred, it stands on a site which is all but the noblest by nature, and which surpasses the sites of all other Northumbrian fortresses in ancient and abiding interest. At Bamburgh above all we are pilgrims come to do our service at one of the great cradles of our national life. Round Bamburgh and its founder, Ida, all Northumbrian history gathers." – FREEMAN

Bamburgh is a natural and almost impregnable fortress. It was probably occupied by the Romans but comes into history as a Celtic stronghold called Dinguaroy. Legend links it with the site of King Arthur's Joyous Garde. In 547 it was seized by the English chieftain Ida, who, the *Anglo-Saxon Chronicle* informs us, "timbered Bamburgh which was at first enclosed by a hedge and afterwards by a wall". The story of Ida is probably a legend, since the quotation above was added to the *Chronicle* at a later date, but it was his grandson Ethelfrith who bestowed Bamburgh on his wife Bebba and from her Bamburgh derives its name (Bebban-burgh). Twice was Bamburgh besieged by the Mercian King Penda. On the first occasion he tried to set fire to the wooden walls and legend says the winds were changed by the miraculous intervention of Aidan who was then resident on the nearby island of Inner Farne. Here, at Bamburgh, was preserved the head and hand of St Oswald, Oswald being for many years the most important local saint until the monks of Durham developed the cult of St Cuthbert.

An early chronicle describes what Bamburgh was like in the 8th century: "Bebba is a most strongly fortified city not very large, being of the size of two or three fields, having one entrance hollowed out of the rock and raised in steps after a marvellous fashion. On the top of the hill it has a church of extremely beautiful workmanship, in which is a shrine rich and costly, that contains wrapt in a pall, the right hand of St Oswald the king still incorrupt as is related by Beda the historian of this nation. To the west on the highest point of the city itself there is a spring of water, sweet to the taste and most pure to the sight, that has been excavated with astonishing labour".

In Anglian times, of course, Bamburgh was really a communal fortress, not as in Norman times a private stronghold. Before 1066 the population was of one race and mainly free. The Normans were foreign conquerors who had reduced the English to a position of serfdom. Their castles therefore were private fortifications primarily intended to defend themselves against their own serfs.

With the decline of the kingdom of Northumbria the castle of Bamburgh slowly decayed, and in the 10th century was twice stormed and pillaged by the Danes. As final proof of its decline in the next century the right hand of St Oswald was stolen by a monk (the head had been purloined 300 years earlier) and the monkish chronicler thus laments its ultimate disgrace. "The city," he says, "renowned formerly for the magnificent splendour of her high estate, has in these latter day been burdened with tribute and reduced to the condition of a handmaiden. She who was once the mistress of the cities of Britain has exchanged the glories of her ancient sabbaths for shame and desolation. The crowds that flocked to her festivals are now represented by a few herdsmen. The pleasures her dignity afforded us are past and gone."

Bamburgh Castle appears again on the stage of history in 1095 when Robert of Mowbray, the third Norman earl of Northumberland, revolted. King William Rufus marched north and quickly overran Northumberland, shutting Mowbray up in Bamburgh. Here is the story as told simply in the *Anglo-Saxon Chronicle*:

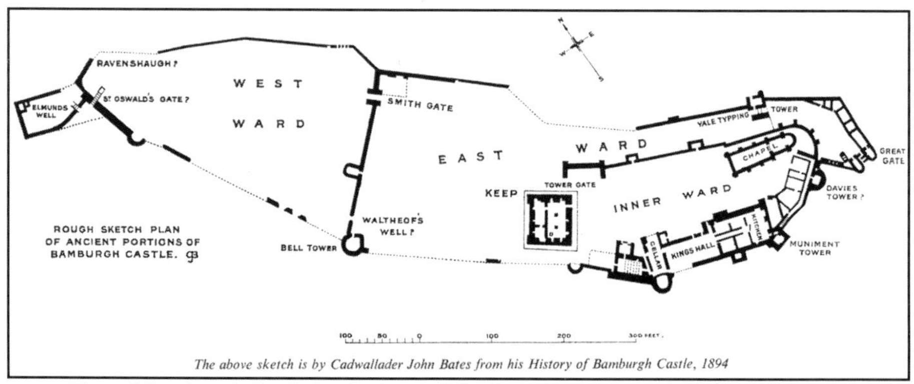

Plan of Bamburgh Castle by C.J.Bates from his History of Bamburgh Castle*, 1894*

"And then at Easter held the king his court at Winchester, and the Earl Robert of Northumberland would not come to court. And the king was much stirred to anger with him for this, and sent to him, and bade him harshly, if he would be worthy of protection, that he would come to court at Pentecost. Hereafter at Pentecost was the king at Windsor, and all his council with him, except the Earl of Northumberland; for the king would neither give him hostages, nor own upon truth, that he might come and go with security. And the king therefore ordered his army and went against the Earl to Northumberland; and soon after he came thither, he won many and nearly all the best of the earl's clan in a fortress, and put them into custody; and the castle at Tinemouth he beset until he won it, and the earl's brother therein, and all that were with him; and afterwards went to Bamborough, and beset the earl therein. But when the king saw that he could not win it, then ordered he his men to make a castle before Bamborough and called it in his speech 'Malveisin', that is in English, 'Evil Neighbour'. And he fortified it strongly with his men, and afterwards went southward. Then, soon after that the king was gone south, went the earl one night out of Bamborough towards Tinemouth; but they that were in the new castle were aware of him, and went after him, and fought him, and wounded him, and afterwards took him. And of those that were with him some they slew, and some they took alive. The king gave orders to take the Earl Robert of Northumberland, and lead him to Bamborough, and put out both his eyes, unless they that were therein would give up the castle. His wife held it, and Morel who was steward, and also his relative. Through this was the castle then given up."

The history of Bamburgh Castle during the Middle Ages is not of great interest. It was only one among many Border fortresses and by no means as important as Alnwick. It was however rebuilt and strengthened and maintained in a position of defence.

In the 17th century the castle came into the hands of the Forster family who squandered their estates with such reckless extravagance that they became bankrupt and their lands were put up for sale. The purchaser, in 1704, was Nathaniel Crewe, Bishop of Durham. Lord Crewe was a notorious timeserving bishop "neither a brilliant political nor ecclesiastical character and there was nothing in his life became him like the leaving of it, since he then founded the Bamburgh Trust".

Lord Crewe died childless and the wealth he had amassed during his life was given to charities which have preserved his name. Archdeacon Sharp, the most famous of the trustees of these charities, administered them well. He restored the castle, established a girls' school there, and made it a centre for aid to shipwrecked sailors.

However, near the end of the 19th century the *Northumberland County History* drew attention to the unsatisfactory state of the castle at that time. "Considering the great historical associations of Bamburgh," they wrote, "considering too the interest of what is left of her ancient architecture and the munificence of the endowments that were intended to raise again her fallen dignity, it cannot honestly be said that the present state of the castle is satisfactory. The girls' school, the presence of which prevents many visitors from seeing the most interesting portion of the castle, would in every way be far better situated near the village, while the array of smoke-cowls that ruin the skyline of the keep, and the numerous sanitary contrivances that disfigure its walls show how ill-fitted it is for a residence and how expensive must be its maintenance as such. A great improvement might be effected at a small cost by knocking off the pasteboard battlements of the castle. The keep should be relieved of its modern fittings and be preserved as a historical monument. The great hall and the buildings connected with it require on the other hand to be plainly restored; and the whole castle, instead of experiencing perhaps some worse fate in store for it, should be made use of for purposes in harmony with the wishes of Lord Crewe, and consonant with its being the pride and glory of the people of Northumberland."

Shortly after these words were written the castle was purchased by the first Lord Armstrong and restored and rebuilt at considerable expense. We might only mention that the result of this restoration was strongly criticized by many antiquarians, historians and architects. But the majestic outline of the castle as seen today is attractive from whatever angle it is viewed and the casual visitor is not particularly disturbed at the rebuilding he sees inside.

The Castle Today

The entrance to Bamburgh Castle is from the south east by a winding road leading up to a strong barbican. The outer gate is guarded by two flanking towers. Beyond is a passage cut through the rock leading to the inner bailey. On the way we pass under the Constable Tower which commands the whole entrance. The area inside covers eight acres.

In the inner bailey stands the great keep, which is earlier in date than the keep at Newcastle. The walls are massive, being over 3m (11 feet) thick on the front, and 2.75m (9 feet) on the other sides. The stone with which it was built was quarried at North Sunderland and they are unusually small. This was to facilitate easy portage by men or pack animals.

The keep is entered by a nail-studded door beneath a fine decorated Norman arch. It leads into a gloomy vaulted room on the ground floor. Hanging on the walls are two huge chains, jokingly called 'King Ida's watch-chains'. They were formerly used for raising sunken vessels. This was done by passing them under the wrecks and buoying them at each end.

In one room of the basement is a remarkable well, 46m (150 feet) deep; half of the distance has been cut through basalt and the remainder through sandstone. It is much older than the keep, probably dating from the 8th century. Simeon of Durham, a monk who wrote in the early 12th century says, "There is in the western side, and in the highest part of the city, a fountain hollowed out in a marvellous fashion, and the water of which is sweet to drink and most limpid to the sight". The wicked queen who, in the ballad of the *Laidley Worm*, changed her stepdaughter into a loathsome worm is said to reside at the bottom of this well in the shape of a toad. Once every seven years she is supposed to reappear.

A mural staircase leads to the upper storeys. On the first floor is the Court Room. In this room are portraits of the two Dorothy Forsters; the first became Lady Crewe, and her niece was the heroine of Walter Besant's novel called *Dorothy Forster* which deals with the abortive revolt of 1715.

Another large vaulted chamber is the armoury containing a great variety of old weapons, and another room houses the library.

Originally the Norman keep was more inhospitable than today. It was intended to serve as a final refuge in case the rest of the castle was captured or the garrison revolted. It was Dr Sharp who first made alterations so that the keep could be permanently habitable.

From the top of the keep magnificent views can be seen taking in Berwick, Holy Island, the Farne Islands, Dunstanburgh Castle and the Cheviot Hills.

At the south east corner once stood the ancient Chapel of St Peter founded in the reign of Henry II. At the north end is a windmill where barley, oats and peas used to be ground for the poor of the district. On the south side are a whole range of buildings. They were erected by Lord Armstrong when he restored the castle.

The main entrance to Bamburgh Castle

ST AIDAN'S CHURCH, BAMBURGH

The parish church of St Aidan is among the finest in Northumberland. It probably stands on the site of the church where St Aidan died, but of that Saxon structure nothing remains. The square tower at the west end belongs to the 13th century but the most striking feature is the very large nave with two arcades of four arches dating from about 1200. The chancel is unusually long and more elaborate, and it has a fine blind arcade of lancet arches running around the upper part of the walls. On the north wall is a piscina [stone basin] under a pointed arch, which drained into the churchyard. Also on the north side is a low side window – a narrow opening through which people who suffered from infectious diseases could receive the communion. On the south side are three graceful sedilia [three stone seats for priests] with trefoiled heads.

The most interesting feature of Bamburgh Church is the 13th century vaulted crypt beneath the chancel, which was either the home of a recluse or used for the exhibition of relics, probably connected with St Aidan. It consists of two chambers on the dividing wall of which a Saxon sundial has been inserted. This crypt was discovered by accident in 1837 when repairs were being made in the chancel.

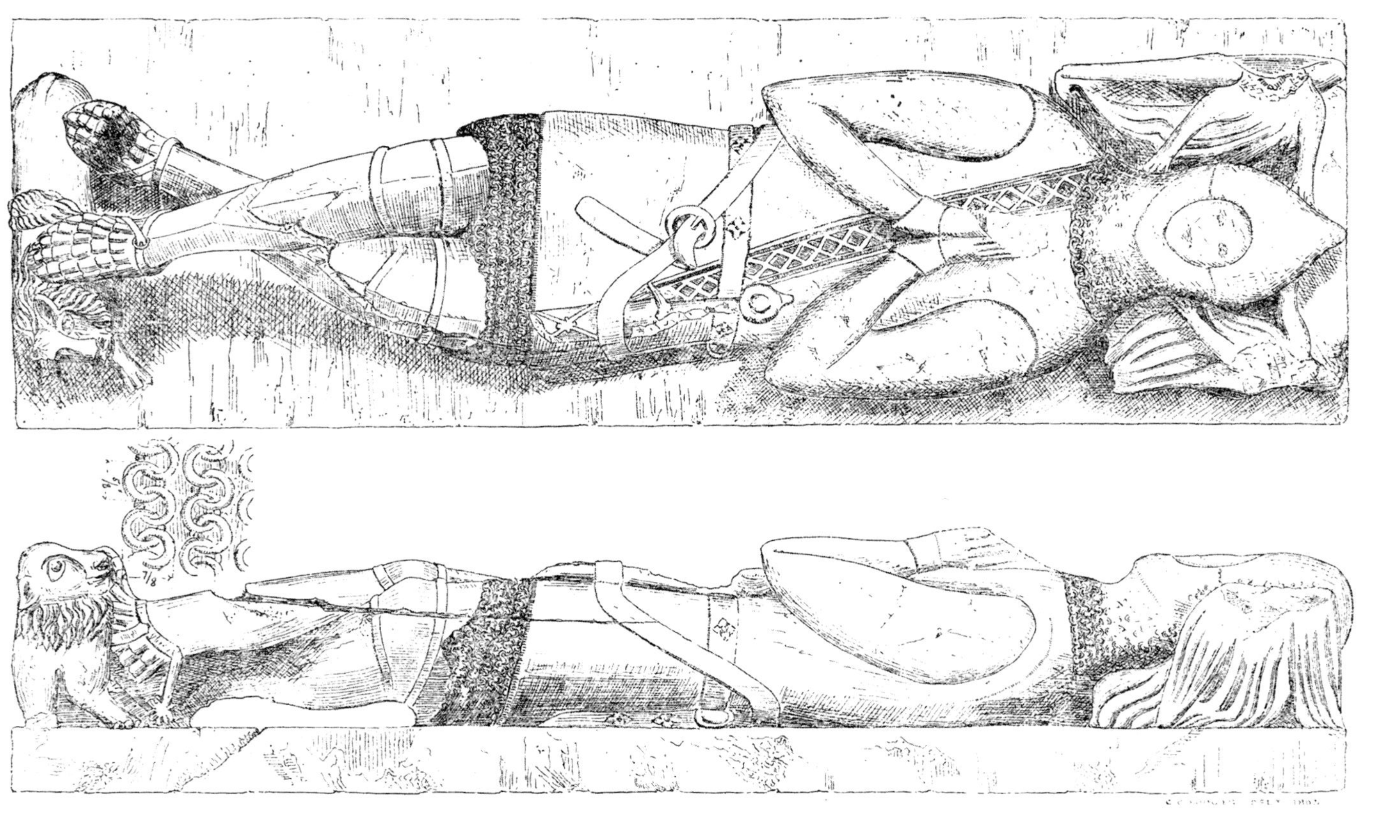

above - 13th Century effigy of a knight in Bamburgh church — Northumberland County History

previous page - Crypt of Bamburgh church

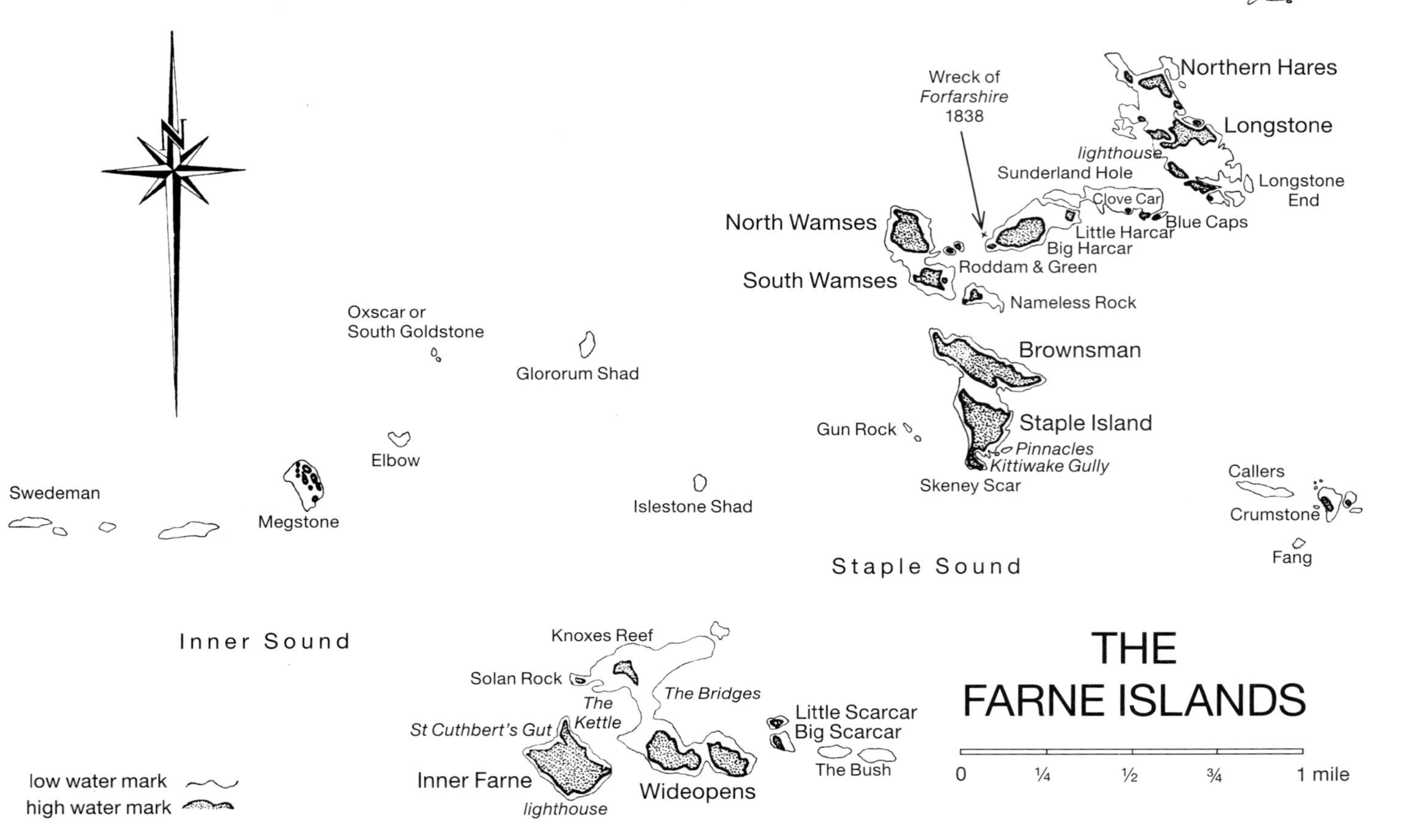

THE
FARNE ISLANDS
N
Knivestone
Northern Hares
Longstone
lighthouse
Longstone
End
Wreck of
Forfarshire
1838
Sunderland Hole
Clove Car
Blue Caps
Little Harcar
Big Harcar
North Wamses
South Wamses
Roddam & Green
Nameless Rock
Brownsman
Staple Island
Pinnacles
Kittiwake Gully
Skeney Scar
Gun Rock
Callers
Crumstone
Fang
Oxscar or
South Goldstone
Glororum Shad
Elbow
Swedeman
Megstone
Islestone Shad
Staple Sound
Inner Sound
Knoxes Reef
Solan Rock
The
Kettle
The Bridges
St Cuthbert's Gut
Inner Farne
lighthouse
Wideopens
Little Scarcar
Big Scarcar
The Bush
0
¼
½
¾
1 mile
low water mark
high water mark

THE FARNE ISLANDS

The Farne Islands, which are chiefly naked rocks, varying in number from fifteen to twenty-eight according to the state of the tide, take their name from the largest which lies nearest to the mainland.

The name Farne is derived from the Celtic *ferann* meaning 'land'. From an ancient document we find that the names of the islands were almost the same in the 13th century as today. They are the most easterly portion of the Great Whin Sill. This formation of igneous rock runs from High Force on the Tees through Durham and Northumberland reaching the sea coast at Cullernose Point where it appears as a vertical cliff. It then bends northward forming the rocks of the coastline as far as Dunstanburgh Castle. It reappears at Embleton and then leaves the mainland forming the Farne Islands. It re-enters the mainland at Bamburgh Castle. The Whin Sill is mainly hard dolerite of about 30m (100 feet) thickness, columnar and fissured. The columnar characteristics can be seen at the Stack which is a monolith 18m (60 feet) in height rising from the sea on the south cliff of the Inner Farne as well as at the Pinnacles which, three in number, are to be found on the south-east of Staple Island. Large fissures can be seen on the Inner Farne at St Cuthbert's Gut and the Churn. At the Churn, when a storm rises, the water rushes up the channel and rises through a blow hole to a height of 30m (100 feet).

A number of the rocks are rounded due to glacial action and deposits of boulder clay on the Inner Farne, Staple Island, Brownsman and the West Wideopens have created layers of soil which are rich from bird droppings. Sedimentary rocks can only be found on the Brownsman, the Bridges and Nameless Rock.

There are no trees on the islands but a few elder bushes, introduced by the lighthouse keepers, can be seen on the Inner Farne. Although the area of soil is very small there is a wide variety of vegetation. More than seventy plants grow on the Farnes as well as lichens and mosses. Sea campion is the characteristic plant of the islands and it blooms in the summer months. Also found flowering in the summer are pink thrift, sorrel, yellow silverweed and white scurvy grass. The orange flowered *Amsinckia intermedia*, a native of California, is found in a fair sized area of the Inner Farne accidentally introduced by the keepers among poultry feed many years ago.

Until recently the only mammals to be seen on the islands were grey seals and rabbits but in 2009 great excitement was caused when paw prints of an otter were spotted, though the animal itself remained elusive.

Although Aidan was the first to live as a hermit on the island it was the prolonged sojourn of St Cuthbert which made the islands famous. He was followed by a number of hermits about whom little is known apart from the host of miracles which took the place of history in those primitive times. The first was Ethelwald, a monk of Ripon, who lived there from 687 to 699. He was succeeded by Felgeld, for whom Bishop Eadfrid rebuilt Cuthbert's oratory. The next hermit was Elwin who left after a quarrel with one Bartholomew who had also come to live there. After living alone for a while Bartholomew was joined by Thomas de Melsonby, who had been elected Prior of Durham against the wishes of Henry III, and had to take refuge in Farne for his own safety. At first the two hermits quarrelled but after a time lived amicably together.

In the *Life of Bartholomew* written about this time there is an interesting account of the islands. It says that "of the adjacent islands, one supplies hay, another fuel, another (which is the nearest) serves as a burial place for shipwrecked sailors. Here the demons are believed to reside, who were compelled by St Cuthbert to quit his island. The brethren, when enjoying their rest after labour, have seen them on a sudden, clad in cowls and riding upon goats, black in complexion, short in stature, their countenances most hideous, their heads long, the appearance of the whole troop horrible. Like soldiers they brandished in their hands lances, which they darted after the fashion of war. At first the sight of the cross was sufficient to repel their attacks, but the only protection in the end was a circumvallation of straws, signed with the cross and fixed in the sand, around which the devils galloped for a while, and then retired, leaving the brethren to enjoy their victories and their repose".

This is a perfect example of the demonology of the period but hidden in it is probably a reference to the early inhabitants of the area, a few of whom had probably survived as primitive food gatherers, living along the sea shore. The monks, not understanding these people, thought of them as demons.

Shortly after the death of Bartholomew the Convent of Durham turned the hermitage of Farne into a permanent institution and sent two monks there, one of whom was called Magister or Custos and the other his Socius and the hermitage was called the House of Farne. The house became well endowed and comparatively wealthy. The records which have survived throw interesting light on the domestic economy of the monasteries in the Middles Ages. The monks exploited the agricultural and fishing wealth of the islands. They grew crops, kept cattle, collected the birds' eggs, and caught the fish and seals which were found in abundance. Wrecks were a regular source of income. In 1357 they borrowed £2 upon the credit of a wreck not yet broken up. In 1364 £4 was received from another wreck. Seals fetched a high price bearing in mind the value of money in those days. For six 'celys' in 1371 they received 27s. 4d. In the same year they spent 45 shillings in buying a clock (horalogium), a rare treasure at that time.

In the 15th century the monks at Farne became very lax. In 1443 the master was dismissed for "pawning the best chalice and divers spoons, associating with ribalds and travelling over the country in garments rent, torn, and covered with mud". In 1461 John Kirke was rebuked for "haunting a womanse house over ofte a for noon and aftir".

In 1538 the monks of Farne ceased to exist as a corporation on the orders of Henry VIII, and the islands were handed over to the Dean and Chapter of Durham.

During the second half of the 16th and early 17th centuries the tower on the Inner Farne was used as a government fort similar to the one on Holy Island. In the reign of Charles II a lighthouse was established, consisting of a coal fire which was lit each night on top of Prior Castell's Tower. It was replaced in the 18th century by a beacon on the Brownsman. At last in 1809 a modern lighthouse with oil lights was established on the Inner Farne. The present lighthouse on Inner Farne is automatic.

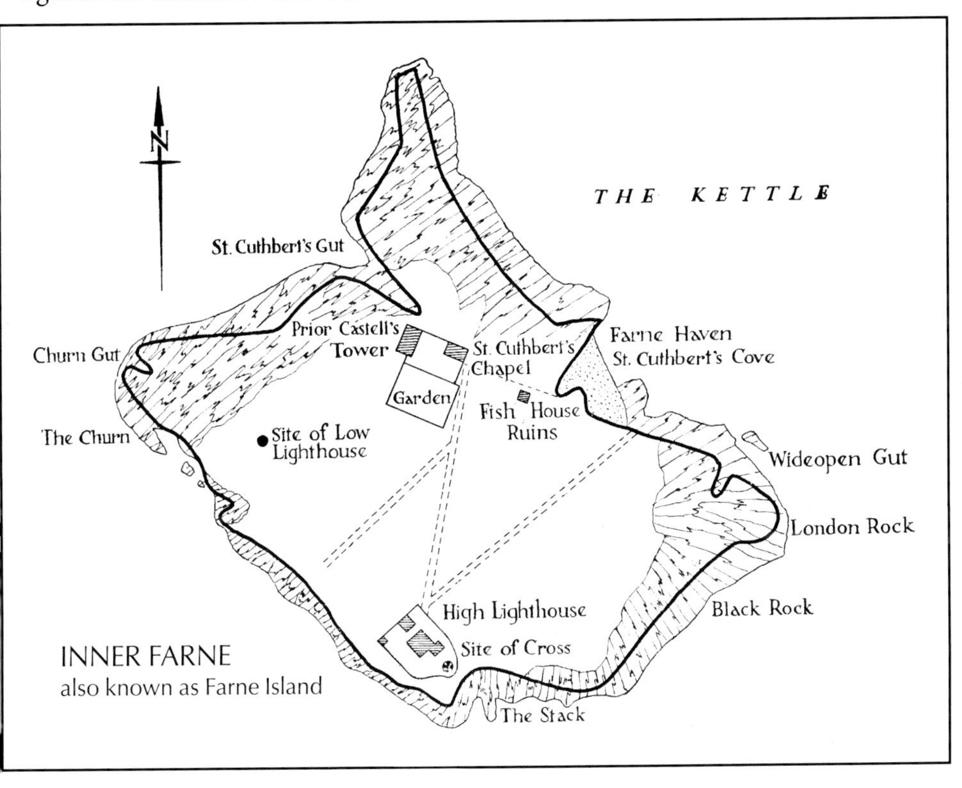

INNER FARNE
also known as Farne Island

Inner Farne

Inner Farne, or Farne Island as it is sometimes called, is the largest of the Farne Group. It is sixteen acres at low tide, but eleven of these are almost entirely bare rock. On the west and south rise steep basalt cliffs 24m (80 feet) high. Five acres are covered with a peaty soil which supports a variety of plants.

On the island are no remains prior to the 14th century with the possible exception of the well. When he lived on the islands St Cuthbert built a cell for himself and a guest house or *hospitium* for visiting monks, together with a well and a cross. The cell and well were probably on the site of Prior Castell's Tower, the only place on the island where there is a well today. Near the landing place stand the meagre remains of an old building, described in Speed's map (1611) as the 'Fishe-house'. This was probably the *hospitium*. In the 14th century there were two chapels on the Farne, one dedicated to St Mary, the other to St Cuthbert. Of St Mary's little remains, but St Cuthbert's (built in 1370) was restored by Archdeacon Thorpe in 1848. Extensive alterations were carried out and of the medieval building only part of the walls and a window in the south wall survive. The interior was decorated with some fine 17th century woodwork brought from Durham Cathedral.

The tower was built by Thomas Castell, Prior of Durham, about 1500. It is a typical Border pele, originally of four storeys. It has a vaulted under-storey and stone staircases, partly spiral. The so-called well of St Cuthbert is on the ground floor, the normal place in a pele tower.

Eastward of Inner Farne are the Wedums or Wideopens, and the Knoxes. At low water they form an island. Nearly a mile north-westward of Inner Farne are two rocks, the Swedman and Megstone.

The inner group of islands is separated from the outer group by the mile wide Staple Sound. Though the sound is deep enough for large ships the two entrances are made dangerous by the Oxscar and the Crumstone.

Staple Island and the Brownsman have extensive remains of two lighthouses on them. The Wamses and Harcars are mainly rocks. The Longstone is a group of islands completely washed by the sea in rough weather. Here in 1826 was built the lighthouse which still exists.

In 1861 the Inner Group of the Farnes was sold by the Dean and Chapter to Archdeacon Thorpe and in 1894 the Outer Group passed into the hands of Lord Armstrong. All the islands were purchased in 1925 for the National Trust.

Sanctuary for Seabirds

Today the Farne Islands are chiefly famous as a bird sanctuary. During the breeding season they are a bird lover's paradise. Some of the birds which breed here are eiders, cormorants, shags, oyster-catchers, terns, herring-gulls, kittiwakes, guillemots and puffins.

Eiders have bred for centuries on the Farnes and are sometimes called St Cuthbert's Duck (or locally, Cuddy's Duck) because they were his favourite birds. They are exceedingly tame in the breeding season and remain on their nest no matter how closely approached.

The male is a black and white bird with green feathers on each side of the head. The female is reddish brown crossed with waved black lines. At the end of June the drakes moult. The eider duck lays from three to six large, smooth, pale olive coloured eggs; these she deposits in a nest made of great quantities of the soft down plucked from her own breast. The foundation of the nest is formed of bent-grass, sea-weeds, or such-like coarse material. The drake plays no part in parenting and leaves to join the other males. When the ducklings have hatched they are looked after by the duck and aunts (non-breeding females). On average there are about 700 breeding pairs on the islands.

Kittiwakes breed in large numbers and prefer rocky promontories and precipices. They can best be seen in Kittiwake Gully on Staple Island. The kittiwake derives its name from its familiar call. Although it resembles the herring-gull it can be distinguished by its smaller size, yellow bill and black legs. It normally lays two eggs which are pale buff blotched with grey or brown. In recent years the number of breeding pairs has declined from over 6000 to about 4000.

Many **puffins**, breed on the Farnes. They are found on all the islands which have sufficient depth of earth in which to make a burrow where they hatch their eggs.

Locally they are called 'Tommy Noddies' because of the amusing way in which they nod their heads when walking. They have large brightly coloured beaks. Their back, crown and a band round the neck is black with white underparts and cheeks. Their legs and feet are orange. The female lays one whitish coloured egg and over 30,000 pairs nest on the Inner Farne, Brownsman, Staple Island, and the Wideopens.

" Visitors often look for puffin nests and are surprised when they cannot find them among those of other birds. This is because the puffin nests underground in old disused rabbit burrows, or in holes excavated by them with their large powerful beaks. The burrows are usually 1 – 1.5m (3 – 5 feet) in length, varying in depth according to the depth of soil available. On one of the islands, wreckage from a wooden ship provides tunnels about 23cms (9 inches) square and the puffins use these as artificial burrows.

"Puffins first visit the islands during February and March as though checking on their nesting sites. They return in early April to claim their burrows and defend them against other would-be occupiers. During this period pairs of puffins can be so engrossed in fighting over the ownership of a burrow, that one can approach within inches of them without being noticed. As the birds are usually paired off before arriving at the breeding site, the only courtship display seen on the land is occasional bill shaking and bowing. Puffins normally lay only one egg and this is incubated by both the birds in turn, for a period of 42 days before the chick is hatched out.

"Both the parents feed the chick and can be seen entering the burrow with several sand eels or small fry in their beaks. The fish are usually lined up in the beak with all the heads on one side and the tails at the other. After about 40 days the young are deserted by the parents and, after being without food for a few days, they are forced to emerge from their burrows. They do this at night and fly away from the islands to fend for themselves on the sea. This is the reason you never see a young puffin on, or near, the islands.

"Puffins have a lot of predators waiting to steal their catch of fish while they are carrying it back to feed their young. Terns can often be seen diving at puffins which are just surfacing with a bill full of fish, forcing them to submerge again. They repeat this so often that the puffin is forced to surrender its catch. Landing on the islands is just as perilous for the puffin as it has to avoid lesser black-backed and herring gulls which wait near the entrance to its burrow and force it to drop the fish. However, observations made at two separate colonies, one where predation of food was heavy and the other where little or no predation took place, showed that the fledgeling puffins in both colonies were of similar weight. This would seem to imply that the adults must compensate for any loss of food. Predation also takes place when gulls seize young puffins which venture too near the entrance of the burrow.

"If puffins burrow in shallow soil, difficulties may arise following a period of dry weather. During such a period the vegetation dies off, exposing the soil to the elements. Rain can then quickly percolate between the soil particles flooding the burrow beneath. Thus any eggs present are chilled, whilst any chicks are forced to flee out of the burrow only to be picked off as they emerge, by waiting gulls.

"The birds are present on and around the islands from February to mid August when they leave to spend the winter months on the oceans."–P.HAWKEY

The **shag** is very like the cormorant, though smaller in size, and is often called the green cormorant. It's colour is metallic green and it lacks the white on chin and thighs; it also wears a crest on the head. It is found on the Inner Farne, Brownsman and Staple Island where it lays two to five chalky coloured eggs. In the early years of the 20th century only odd pairs nested on the islands. Now a 1000 nesting pairs is about average. Unlike the cormorant the shag will defend its nest and doesn't breed in a colony.

The **cormorant** is a large bird measuring some 90cms (36 inches) in length. It has webbed feet and a long bill of which the upper mandible is hooked and sharp. The colour is glossy blue black in front and bronze brown on the back. The female lays three or more greenish white eggs. Being timid birds they gather in colonies for protection and their nesting area smells of decaying fish. The number of breeding pairs is now about half of the 300 recorded around 1970.

Shag

Herring-gull and guillemot colony

Crowds of noisy and squabbling **guillemots** are to be found on the Pinnacles. They deposit their eggs on the narrowest of ledges and the over-crowding on the top of the three basaltic columns has to be seen to be believed. The guillemot is 46cms (18 inches) in length, darkish brown in colour with white underparts. It is an ocean bird rarely seen near land except when breeding. One egg is laid on bare rock, this is pear shaped so that when it is knocked it revolves. There are almost 50,000 guillemots on the islands.

In 1971 ten pairs of **razorbills** bred on the Farne Islands, mainly on the Inner Farne. Since then their numbers have shown a steady increase and there are now over 300 breeding pairs. The plumage is black with white underparts and a white bar on the wing. It is distinguishable from the guillemot mainly by its beak which is shorter and flattened with a white grooved line across the bill. The female lays a single egg on the bare rock. In the winter the birds feed and roost on the sea.

The **arctic tern** is the most common bird on the Farnes, several thousand pairs breed annually. The mantle and underpart are pale grey, the crown black, the bill and legs red. Three eggs, laid in a shallow scrape, is a full clutch. The colours are often different for each egg. They nest on the Brownsman, Inner Farne and Staple Island.

Despite its name the **common tern** is rare on the Farne Islands. Their numbers fluctuate considerably [say, 100 – 200 pairs]. They are sometimes called 'sea swallows'. Difficult to distinguish from the arctic tern their bill is sharper and orange in colour.

The **sandwich tern** is the largest of the family and is often called the 'big tern'. It may be distinguished from the other terns by its black legs and feet, and black bill with yellow tip. About 1,500 pairs breed on the Farnes but their location varies. They normally lay two eggs without even a scrape for nest and their eggs are pale buff spotted with brown.

The **herring-gull and lesser black-backed gull** are much the same size. The herring-gull is white with pale grey mantle, black wing tips, pink legs and yellow bill. The lesser black-backed gull has a very dark mantle and yellow legs. Both birds are a nuisance since they devour eggs and young birds. The wardens therefore collect as many of their eggs as can be found to keep their numbers down. There are approximately 500 pairs of each species breeding on most of the islands.

The **oyster-catcher** is a wader and in spite of its name mainly eats limpets, not oysters. It is glossy black on the head, back and upper breast, and white underneath with a bright scarlet bill. They lay three eggs, greenish-grey in colour and spotted with black, on the shingle or rock. About 35 pairs breed annually.

Fulmar petrels have a white plumage with a grey mantle and tail. The female lays one large white egg only, which she hatches on a rocky ledge. Fulmars were first seen at the Farnes in 1919 but for a long time only odd pairs nested. Now over 200 pairs are to be found.

Bird Protection on the Farne Islands

Arrow heads found on the islands show that primitive man probably hunted the wildlife on the Farne Islands for food but, when St Cuthbert inhabited Inner Farne in 676, he protected the nesting eiders, and this is the earliest record of protection on the islands. St Cuthbert died in 687 but successive hermits continued this protection of the eider. Other birds and their eggs, however, were used for food or sold to the people on the mainland, and seals were killed for food and oil. Because of this exploitation the seal and bird populations must have been considerably smaller than they are today.

During the occupation of the islands by the monks from 1255 to 1536, records in Durham show that birds and eggs were eaten and sold and this exploitation was continued by successive tenants, after the dissolution of the monasteries, until 1831 when Archdeacon Thorp of Durham employed

above - King Egfrid visits Cuthbert on Inner Farne and asks him to accept Bishopric of Lindisfarne.

right - Farne Island Tower, c.1790

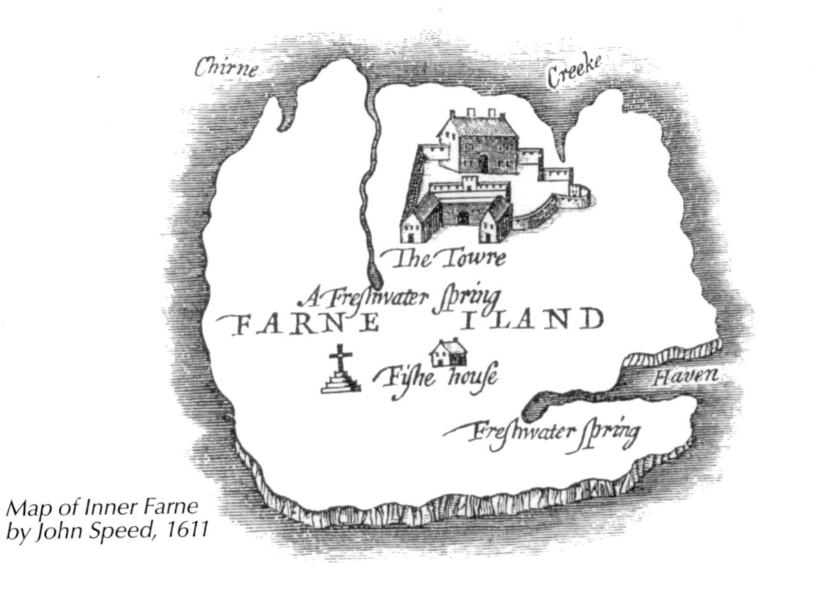

Map of Inner Farne
by John Speed, 1611

watchers to look after the birds during the breeding season. After his death in 1862 the islands were left again without protection until 1880 when the first-ever Bird Protection Act was passed by Parliament.

Following a successful public appeal for funds the islands were purchased and handed over to the National Trust in 1925, to be maintained as a bird sanctuary forever. The National Trust wardens live on the islands from March to December. Home for them is the 15th century pele tower on Inner Farne or the old lighthouse keeper's cottage on Brownsman.

How to get to the Farnes

The starting point is Seahouses harbour. From here regular boat trips are available in the spring and summer. Landings are allowed from the beginning of April until the end of October. Only Inner Farne and Staple Island are open to the public.

The Grey Seal

The Farne Islands are an important breeding-place on the east coast of Britain of the grey seal. St Cuthbert is often depicted with the grey seal. In medieval times and until a century ago large numbers were killed at the Farnes mainly for the oil which could be extracted from their bodies. In the early 1900s there were only about 100 seals in the colony and the Grey Seal Act of 1932 was passed to protect them. Thereafter their numbers greatly increased.

The colony became too large and in 1966 a fair number had to be killed. By 1970 with over 7,000 seals, of which 2,000 were breeding cows, their numbers were once again causing trouble. On some islands they had destroyed the top soil and vegetation and they themselves had become so overcrowded in their breeding grounds that disease was rife. Today, with careful management and without culling, their numbers and nursery sites are controlled. Storms also play a part in limiting numbers. On average half of the pups born on the Farnes die before they are three weeks old.

Grey seals are larger than common seals. The bulls, usually dark in colour, can measure 3m in length and weigh over 290kg (over 600 pounds) The cows are smaller, being grey on the upper parts with patches of cream underneath. The seals calve in October and November, their nurseries being mainly on Brownsman, Staple Island and the two Wamses. The pups are cream at birth and weigh about 13kg (30 pounds). However, they quickly increase in weight since seal's milk is very rich. Within ten days they moult and by five weeks they have their second coat which is usually grey. A month after its birth the weaned pup takes to the sea to fend for itself. After weaning the adults mate, the pregnancy lasts just over eleven months.

The seals are a common sight and can often be seen either hauled out on the rocks or investigating visiting boats.

14th Century St Cuthbert's chapel

An engraving of Grace Darling along with the coble she and her father used in the Forfarshire rescue.

GRACE DARLING

Grace Horsley Darling was born at Bamburgh on the 24th November, 1815. Her home is still standing. Her paternal grandfather came from Scotland and settled down at Belford, near Bamburgh, as a cooper. On her mother's side Grace was descended from the Northumbrian family of the Horsleys. The Horsleys were once great people in Bamburgh. In the year 1323 one Roger de Horsley had been constable of Bamburgh Castle. The Horsleys had owned land in the area but their fortunes had declined by the 17th century. Her father, William Darling, was a lighthouse keeper on the Brownsman and here she spent the first ten years of her life. In 1826 the family moved to the newly built Longstone Light.

On the Longstone Grace Darling lived a quiet and secluded life, assisting her father and her mother in their work. One of her interests was natural history which was fostered by her father who was an authority on the bird life of the Farnes. Many specimens for the newly formed Natural History Museum in Newcastle were provided by him. Although Grace had six brothers and sisters, they had all, except for a brother who died, settled on the mainland.

On 7th September, 1838, the wreck of the *Forfarshire* was an event which was to change the whole of Grace Darling's life. Many accounts have been written of this famous episode but none is better than the simple description to be found in William Darling's Journal.

"SEPT. 5. The steamboat *Forfarshire*, 400 tons, sailed from Hull for Dundee on the 6th, at midnight. When off Berwick, her boilers became so leaky as to render her engine useless. Captain Humble then bore away for Shields; blowing strong gale, north, with thick fog. About 4 a.m. on the 7th the vessel struck the west point of Harker's rock, and in fifteen minutes broke through by the paddle axle, and drowned forty-three persons; nine having previously left in their own boat, and were picked up by a Montrose vessel, and carried to Shields and nine others held on by the wreck and were rescued by the Darlings. The cargo consisted of superfine cloths, hardware, soap, boiler plate, and spinning gear. The North Sunderland boat got to the wreck about 10 a.m.; and after carrying the body of Rev. Mr. Robb and two children, with some other things, to the high part of the rock, came away and with some difficulty got into Sunderland Hole, Longstone, and launched their boat over the rocks into safety, there being no possibility of pulling their boat into the haven of Longstone, and had to stop in the old barracks two days and nights with scant provisions, no beds and no change of cloths."

Grace Darling and her father returning from the wreck of the Forfarshire, by J.W.Carmichael

Trinity House asked for further details and William Darling sent the following letter:

"DEAR SIR, In answer to your request of 29th ult., I have to state that on the morning of the 7th September, it blowing gale with rain from the north, my daughter and me being both on the alert before high water securing things out of doors, one quarter before five my daughter observed a vessel on the Harker's rock; but owing to the darkness, and spray going over her, could not observe any person on the wreck although the glass was incessantly applied, until near seven o'clock when, the tide being fallen, we observed three or four men upon the rock: we agreed that if we could get to them some of them would be able to assist us back, without which we could not return, and having no idea of a possibility of a boat coming from North Sunderland, we immediately launched our boat, and was enabled to gain the rock, where we found eight men and one woman, which I judged rather too many to take at once in the state of the weather, therefore took the woman and four men to the Longstone. Two of

Grace Darling's birthplace, Bamburgh

them returned with me, and succeeded in bringing the remainder, in all nine persons safely to the Longstone about nine o'clock. Afterwards the boat from North Sunderland arrived and found three lifeless bodies."

The *Forfarshire* was one of the early paddle steamers and her loss aroused public interest, since the owners were accused of negligence. The first inquest at Bamburgh passed the following verdict – "Wrecked on board the *Forfarshire* steam packet by the imperfections of the boilers, and the culpable negligence of the captain in not putting back to port. Deodand [a fine] on the vessel, £100".

The publicity given to the inquest, and the scandal of the ship's condition, there presumed to have been proved, was of material importance in stimulating the demand for regular inspection of all steamships and the granting of certificates of sea-worthiness. The wreck of the *Forfarshire* was, therefore, apart from Grace Darling's role in it, an event of some historical importance. Later a second inquest blamed the weather.

The story of Grace Darling attracted extraordinary interest throughout the country. Modern publicity and commercialism was in its infancy but as soon as the facts of the rescue were reported an avalanche of reporters descended upon Grace Darling. None of the Darlings enjoyed this publicity and many of the stories that were written were so false that a great deal of ill-feeling was raised in the neighbourhood. In one period of twelve days they had to sit to seven different portrait painters. Poems, of an indifferent sort, novels, even worse, paintings and mementoes were produced in abundance. The manager of the Adelphi Theatre in London offered her £10 a week to appear there rowing her boat on the stage. The Humane Society gave them both gold medals. A public subscription raised £750 for Grace and £250 for her father.

Grace continued to live on Longstone with her parents and was ever the object of curious visitors. She succumbed to tuberculosis and died in Bamburgh on 20th October, 1842, aged just twenty-six. She is buried in Bamburgh churchyard where there is a memorial.

The Grace Darling museum at Bamburgh preserves many relics of the Grace Darling mania. There we can see bills advertising trips to the Longstone to gaze on Grace, a beaver bonnet presented by the hat makers of Berwick, a volume of sermons given by the Archdeacon of Northumberland, and a velvet armchair from the Duchess. A lock of her hair, the cup she used, fragments of her dress, and a pair of her slippers are all to be seen. The place of honour in the museum, however, goes to the boat used in the rescue, a Northumberland coble some 6.5m (21½ feet) long.

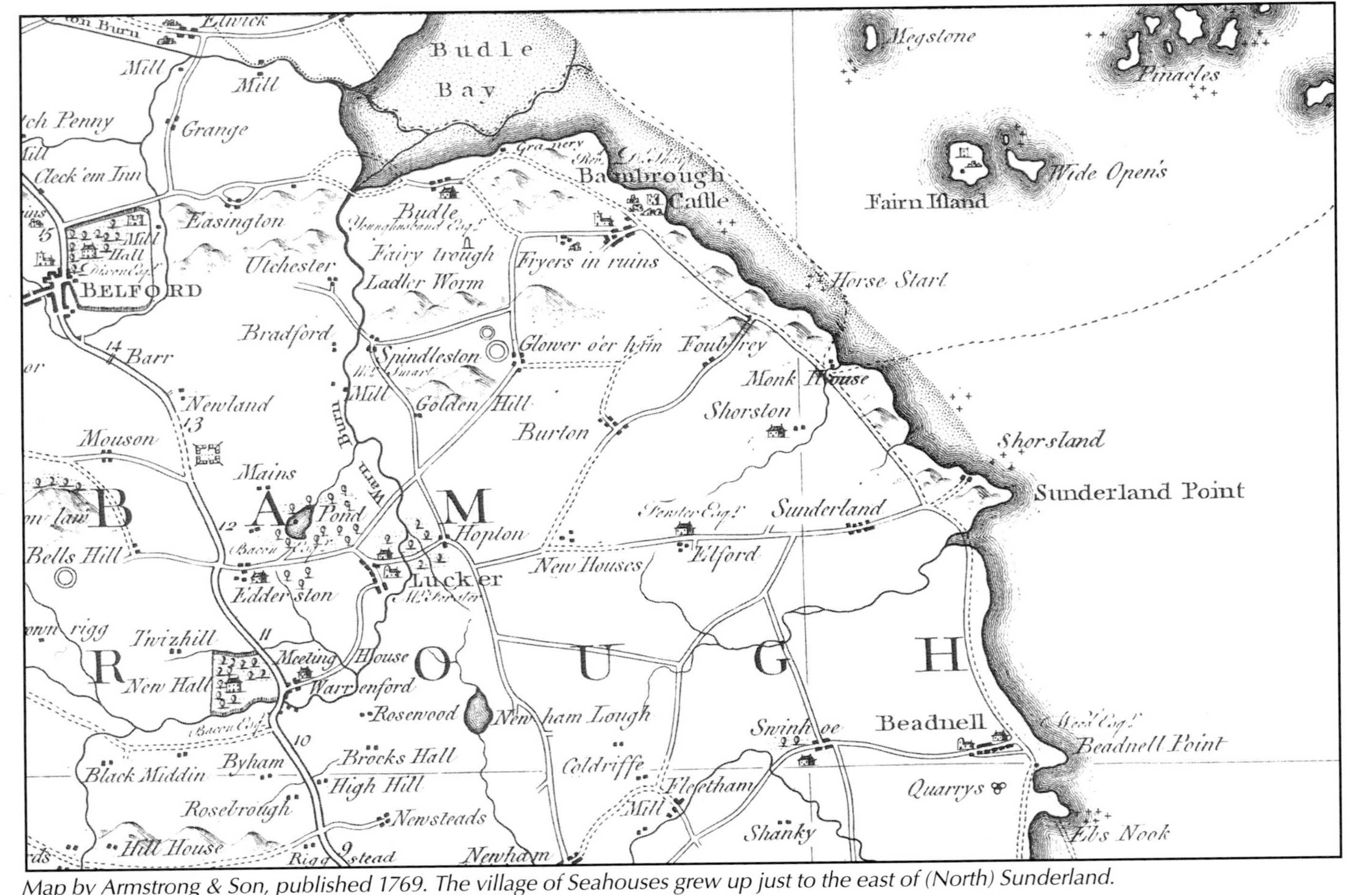

Map by Armstrong & Son, published 1769. The village of Seahouses grew up just to the east of (North) Sunderland.

SOUTH OF BAMBURGH

Monks' House

Between Seahouses and Bamburgh is a group of buildings now called Monks' House. The place was originally named Brocksmouth. In 1257 Henry II granted the monks of Farne Island a small plot of land here on which they built a storehouse for their provisions. This building was called Monks' House. In the 19th century one of the buildings was a tavern called St Cuthbert's Inn.

North Sunderland and Seahouses

North Sunderland and Seahouses lie three miles south of Bamburgh. The older of the two villages is North Sunderland. The name Sunderland means the 'land south of Bamburgh', and in the oldest documents is called 'Sutherlannland'. The contradictory word 'North' was added to avoid confusion with the much larger Sunderland on the river Wear.

The limestone trade was important to both communities and limekilns and then a new harbour were built in the late 1700s. Then, in 1889, with the increasing importance of fishing a further new outer harbour was constructed and the village of Seahouses grew in size. Today it has a resident population of some 1,800. Fishing still goes on but it's the holiday trade that makes Seahouses a busy centre in the summer months.

Initially Seahouses attracted bird-watchers and naturalists who were interested in the Farne Islands. Then in the 1920s holidaymakers came by rail to North Sunderland and by car in the 1950s to caravan parks and b&bs. Today Seahouses is well established as a holiday destination.

above - Seahouses harbour

opposite page - Beadnell harbour and limekilns

Beadnell

A fine stretch of sands extends from Newton Point north to the rocky headland of Ebb's Nook and is known as Beadnell Bay. The village and harbour is near the north end. In the 18th century the Beadnell races, run along the sands, were a popular event until 1794, when one of the riders was killed. The rocky headland is composed of magnesium limestone resting on a bed of shale. There are also sandstone and coal seams running out to sea. There are a number of inlets between the rocks called holes such as Nacker Hole and Collith Hole.

The village was probably established in Saxon times. On the headland of Ebb's Nook the remains of an ancient chapel were discovered in 1853 and the excavations suggest that a building was erected on this spot and dedicated to St Ebba shortly after the introduction of Christianity to Northumberland. The Muster Roll of 1538 lists 71 able-bodied men at Beadnell.

Beadnell was in the 19th century an important fishing village and in the 18th century a great resort for smugglers. One of their secret hideouts, a hidden vault, was discovered on the Farne Islands when the Chapel of St Cuthbert was being restored. One day in September, 1762, the customs officers seized 2,700 gallons of brandy, 400 gallons of rum and geneva, twenty-three hogsheads of wine, and some tea which had been landed by Scottish smugglers.

Beadnell village runs inland from the haven. In the early years of the 18th century it consisted of two rows of houses with a village green in the middle. The chapel on the green was originally built in about 1740 and was then was rebuilt in 1860.

There were five principal houses. On the north side was the East Hall, now Beadnell Hall Hotel, then inhabited by Willam Forster, the largest landowner in the village. It was built in the late 17th century. A tower which once stood on the east end used to belong to the Hardings, a Newcastle family, who settled in Beadnell in 1383. A doorway that once led into the old tower is visible in a cupboard in the east parlour of the hall. In 1735 the hall was purchased by the Wood family. The fine panelling in two of the rooms dates from this period. The outside was gothicized later in the 18th century with castellated gable, typical quatrefoils and sashed windows.

A smaller house was occupied by Richard Taylor. The site is now the Beadnell House Hotel. On the south side was Beadnell Town Farm and on an unknown site was the Black Hall.

Beadnell Tower stood in the centre of the village. This three-storeyed pele-tower is now changed into an inn called The Craster Arms. Beadnell tower was built by the Forster family in the 16th century. By 1818 the old tower had come to serve as the back premises of a public house once called the Bull Inn.

A great deal of the original pele survives. The basement, now used as a beer-cellar, is vaulted, and remains of the newel staircase which led to the next floor can be seen. The walls are over 2.4m (8 feet) thick in places. On the ground floor remains of an old fireplace are visible.

The outside of the pele was restored in the 18th century and there is now a pretty two-bayed frontage adorned with a fine coat of arms and large foliage trails carved in stone. The coat of arms belongs to the Craster family with a raven as crest and the motto, *Dum vivo spero* - 'While there's life there's hope'.

Also attached to the front is the lead sign of a Newcastle insurance company, with the insignia of three castles and the number 7058. In the days before public fire services the fire engines were controlled by insurance companies who only put out fires in buildings bearing their plaque. In the eastern wall of the inn has been inserted the carved head of a man. Its origin is uncertain.

Since the area was important for corn growing a number of granaries were built along the coast. One of them became part of the house called Beadnell Cottage, now the Beadnell Towers Hotel.

In the 18th century Beadnell was isolated and difficult to reach. It was not until 1790 that the road north to Seahouses was made passable by the building of a bridge across the Annstead Burn by John Wood.

The limestone at Beadnell made very good lime and in 1747 the first kilns were built. The lime trade was very profitable and to facilitate export a harbour was built. Limekilns needed coal which fortunately could be found in several seams in the area. Supplies of coal made salt pans a viable proposition and Beadnell was set to become an important town.

Fishing was also expanding and in 1788 John Wood formed here a company called the Northumberland Branch of the British Fishery. But the export of fish, lime and salt made a better harbour a vital necessity. By 1798 the pier had been built and in the same year Richard Pringle built a limekiln on it. By the terms of his lease with John Wood, "Pringle had to build a kiln twenty-four feet high from the kiln eyes to the top, nine feet in diameter within at the bottom, and sixteen feet in diameter at the top. To meet the expense he was to be allowed to have the profit of burning four thousand loads of shell lime. For every load of shell lime sold thereafter, Pringle was to pay ninepence upon each load that he shipped, and sixpence per load on land sales. He pledged himself to ship a thousand loads every year. If more kilns than one should be required (as proved to be the case), Mr Wood was to be at the expense of building them." (Sir Edmund Craster) *Archaeologia Aeliana* (1956)

However, herring fishing soon became more important than the lime trade. We read in 1828 of one thousand fishermen entering Beadnell harbour in a storm. In 1822 the limekilns were no longer used for their original purpose but were turned over to curing herring.

The three limekilns which were then built now belong to the National Trust.

Craster Arms at Beadnell

NORTH AND WEST OF BAMBURGH

Budle

Leaving Bamburgh by a road called the Wynding one comes to the sea shore. Following the sand dunes north for half a mile one comes to the Harkess rocks, a fascinating place for the geologist since they "display almost every vagary to which the igneous rocks are subject". Less than a mile further on is Budle Bay, famous for its cockles. The village of Budle (the word means dwelling) now hardly exists although in the Middle Ages, along with Spindleston, it was a place of greater importance.

Warenmouth

The port of Warenmouth has long since disappeared. At one time it was the most northerly port in England (Berwick then being a Scottish town). It was the port for Bamburgh and could accommodate the largest vessels then afloat. It was built about 1250 by William Heron, the constable of Bamburgh Castle. Henry III granted a charter to the town giving the burgesses the same liberties as those of Newcastle. The name soon fell into disuse and the port was called Newtown. It ceased to be used as a port in the 15th century as Bamburgh itself declined, although a number of fishermen continued to live there. The harbour was protected by a fortified tower. It is mentioned in a deed of 1628 and is shown on a map of Newtown made in 1781 where it is called a 'bastile'. The site of the village is unknown.

Elwick

The township of Elwick borders on Fenham Flats which stretch out towards Holy Island. Until 1844 the northern part belonged to the Bishop of Durham. The old farmhouse was replaced by farm cottages in 1864. In the list of towers, compiled in 1415, two towers are mentioned in Elwick – that of Thomas de Bradforth and that of Thomas de Elwick. The same two towers are mentioned again in 1561.

Ross

The township of Ross has been almost uninhabited since it was turned into pasture about 1556. The land is low and flat and is protected from the sea by the links or sand banks which stretch out towards Holy Island. The northern point which forms the southern barrier of Holy Island Bay is called the Old Law (formerly Rosse-scalpe).

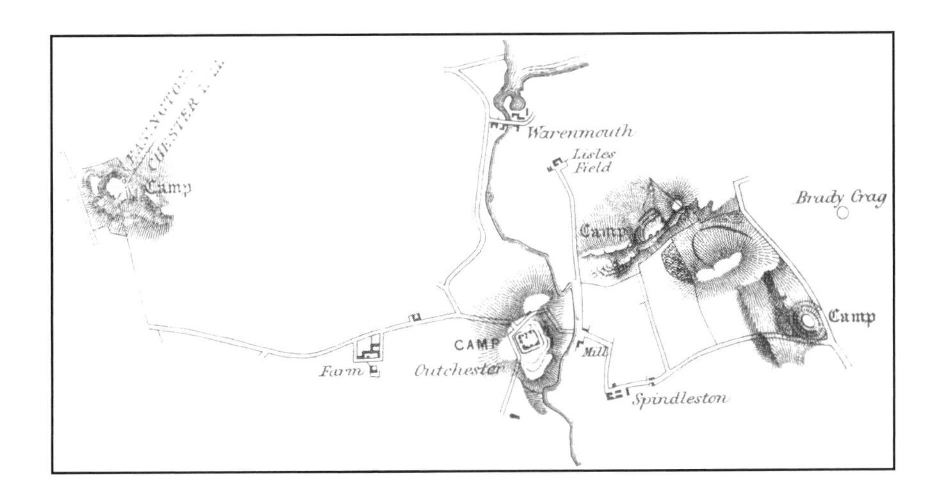

Outchester

The township of Outchester lies at the mouth of the Waren burn. The remains of the camp from which it is named lies on the left bank of the burn. Within the camp is a tall conical stone building, once a windmill, but now called 'The Old Ducket'. The first owner of Outchester was one Bodin at the beginning of the 12th century. In the 15th century the village consisted of two rows of houses called the North-rowe and the South-rowe. There was a tower attached to the manor house but all trace has gone. It is first mentioned in a deed of 1462 and other documents of the period. Some time after 1580 one Thomas Jackson of Berwick, who held a mortgage on the property, expelled the tenants and put the land to pasture, a process very common in Northumberland where most of the farms are descendants of medieval villages. So Outchester disappeared and the site of the village is unknown. The farm of Outchester as seen today is comparatively modern.

Spindleston

The township is wild and picturesque and the Spindleston Heughs form a conspicuous landmark overlooking the low lying coastal lands. The name means spindle-rock, so called from an upstanding pillar of whinstone between the two hills. Here the hero of the ballad of the *Laidley Worm of Spindleston Heugh* is said "to have hung the bridle-rein of his horse as he prepared himself for approaching the den of the worm in the marshy hollow farther up".

The *Laidley Worm of Spindleston Heugh* [laidley means loathsome and worm is an old word for serpent] was published in the 19th century by the

Rev Robert Lamb, vicar of Norham. It was claimed to be from an ancient manuscript, and the work of the mountain bard, Duncan Frasier, living on Cheviot in 1270. The poem is a fake, though how much genuine legend, if any, Robert Lamb worked into his poem is uncertain.

One of the cliffs is called the Cat's Crag because it was once the home of the wild cat. The highest point of the crags (74m / 243 feet) contains a native British camp. Many of the stones from the ramparts have been used for buildings in the neighbourhood but three ramparts can be made out, probably built at different times. About half a mile south is another camp which can barely be traced because of continual ploughing.

cormorant